EQUAL®
SWEETENER

Eating Light

Publications International, Ltd.

Favorite Brand Name Recipes at www.fbnr.com

Photography: Stephen Hamilton Photographics, Inc.
Photographers: Stephen Hamilton, Tate Hunt
Photographers' Assistant: Tom Gadja
Prop Stylist: Paula Walters
Food Stylists: Kim Hartman, Cindy Melin
Assistant Food Stylists: Sara Cruz, Carol Radford

Pictured on the front cover: Lemon Meringue Pie *(page 60)*.

Pictured on the back cover *(clockwise from top left):* Gingered Chicken with Vegetables *(page 28)*, Soy Milk Smoothie *(page 10)* and Cranberry Apple Crisp *(page 82)*.

ISBN-13: 978-1-4127-0258-4
ISBN-10: 1-4127-0258-5

Manufactured in China.

8 7 6 5 4 3 2 1

Microwave Cooking: Microwave ovens vary in wattage. Use the cooking times as guidelines and check for doneness before adding more time.

Questions about Equal? Call toll-free 1-800-323-5316.
Or write to Equal Consumer Affairs, PO Box 1280, South Bend, IN 46624.
For more great recipes and information, visit the Equal web site at **equal.com**

Eating Light

A Better Way to the
   Taste You Love 6

Beverages & Spreads 8

Entrées, Salads & Sides 24

Cookies & Bars 42

Pies & Tarts 52

Cakes & Cheesecakes 66

More Desserts 82

Index 93

A BETTER WAY TO THE TASTE YOU LOVE

It's been more than two decades since Americans were first introduced to the sugar-like taste of Equal® sweetener. We've partnered Equal with our favorite foods—coffee, tea, cereal and fruit—to come away with the taste we love. Since then, Equal sweetener has revolutionized the way we eat—it has become an American classic because it's in a class by itself.

Why use Equal? If you want to limit your sugar intake, reduce calories and minimize carbohydrates, then Equal has the recipes for your success. *Eating Light* introduces you to over 50 delicious recipes for you and your family's enjoyment—from beverages, salads and entrées to a tempting variety of desserts.

You'll find that it's easy to make Equal a part of your daily diet. Equal's test kitchen staff has developed and tested new recipes that offer convenient, delicious, lower in calorie food options that fit into your busy life. Equal can be used instead of sugar in practically any recipe where sugar functions primarily as a sweetener. But keep in mind that while all sugar substitutes sweeten like sugar, their cooking properties are different. In recipes where sugar also provides structure and volume (cakes, brownies, cookies, etc.), some modifications may be required for best results.

With the introduction of a new member to the Equal family—4-ounce Equal® Spoonful—now it's even easier to make Equal a part of your recipes! Equal Spoonful now comes in a large size that's perfect for making multiple recipes. From delicious fruit pies to luscious cheesecakes, Equal Spoonful adds the taste of sugar without all the calories. It measures cup for cup like sugar and comes in a resealable container made for easy pouring and storing. Add it to your pantry along with pre-measured Equal packets and Equal tablets. You'll love the convenience.

EQUAL® SWEETENER CONVERSION CHART

SUGAR	EQUAL® PACKETS	EQUAL® SPOONFUL
2 teaspoons	1 packet	2 teaspoons
1 tablespoon	1½ packets	1 tablespoon
¼ cup	6 packets	¼ cup
⅓ cup	8 packets	⅓ cup
½ cup	12 packets	½ cup
¾ cup	18 packets	¾ cup
1 cup	24 packets	1 cup
1 pound	57 packets	2¼ cups

You'll find essential nutrition information with every recipe, including the percent calorie reduction from a traditional recipe. Nutritional values have been calculated using the basic recipe without garnishes or optional ingredients. When ingredient choices appear in the recipe, the first choice has been used for the nutrition analysis. Dietary exchanges have been calculated and are also based on the basic recipe without garnishes or optional ingredients. The dietary exchanges have been rounded to the nearest half number.

Beverages & Spreads

Cranberry-Lime Margarita Punch

23% calorie reduction from traditional recipe

> 6 **cups water**
> 1 **container (12 ounces) frozen cranberry juice cocktail**
> ½ **cup fresh lime juice**
> ¼ **cup EQUAL® SPOONFUL***
> 2 **cups ice cubes**
> 1 **cup diet ginger ale or tequila**
> 1 **lime, sliced**

*May substitute 6 packets Equal® sweetener.

• Combine water, cranberry juice, lime juice and Equal® in punch bowl; stir until Equal® dissolves.

• Stir in ice cubes, diet ginger ale and sliced lime; garnish with fresh cranberries if desired.   *Makes 10 servings*

Nutrients per Serving:	
Calories:	87
Fat:	0 g
Protein:	0 g
Carbohydrate:	23 g
Cholesterol:	0 mg
Sodium:	9 mg

Dietary Exchanges: 1½ Fruit

Soy Milk Smoothie

28% calorie reduction from traditional recipe

> **3 cups plain or vanilla soy milk**
> **1 banana, peeled and frozen (see Tip)**
> **1 cup frozen strawberries or raspberries**
> **1 teaspoon vanilla or almond extract**
> **⅓ cup EQUAL® SPOONFUL***

*May substitute 8 packets Equal® sweetener.

• Place all ingredients in blender or food processor. Blend until smooth.   *Makes 4 servings*

Tip: Peel and cut banana into large chunks. Place in plastic freezer bag, seal and freeze at least 5 to 6 hours or overnight.

Nutrients per Serving:	
Calories:	147
Fat:	3 g
Protein:	8 g
Carbohydrate:	22 g
Cholesterol:	0 mg
Sodium:	80 mg

Dietary Exchanges: ½ Fruit, 1 Milk, ½ Fat

Equal® Cinnamon Cream Cheese

35% calorie reduction from traditional recipe

8 ounces whipped cream cheese
⅔ cup EQUAL® SPOONFUL*
1¼ teaspoons ground cinnamon

*May substitute 16 packets Equal® sweetener.

• Combine cream cheese with Equal® and cinnamon.

• Spread mixture on bagels, croissants, bread and crackers.

• For variety, stir in 1 or 2 tablespoons of the following: raisins, chopped nuts, mini chocolate chips, chopped fresh apple, dried cherries, dried cranberries, or mixed dried fruits.

Makes 11 servings

Nutrients per Serving (2 tablespoons):	
Calories:	78
Fat:	7 g
Protein:	2 g
Carbohydrate:	2 g
Cholesterol:	23 mg
Sodium:	61 mg

Dietary Exchanges: 1½ Fat

Fruit Smoothies

34% calorie reduction from traditional recipe

> **1 cup orange juice**
> **1 cup fat-free plain yogurt**
> **1 banana, peeled and frozen (see Tip)**
> **1 cup frozen strawberries or raspberries**
> **¼ cup EQUAL® SPOONFUL***

*May substitute 6 packets Equal® sweetener.

• Place all ingredients in blender or food processor. Blend until smooth.   *Makes 2 servings*

Tip: Peel and cut banana into large chunks. Place in plastic freezer bag, seal and freeze at least 5 to 6 hours or overnight.

Nutrients per Serving:	
Calories:	202
Fat:	0 g
Protein:	8 g
Carbohydrate:	45 g
Cholesterol:	3 mg
Sodium:	78 mg

Dietary Exchanges: 2 Fruit, 1 Milk

Peach Freezer Jam

65% calorie reduction from traditional recipe

2 pounds peaches, peeled, pitted and coarsely chopped
1 package (1¾ ounces) no-sugar-needed pectin
1 to 1½ cups unsweetened apple juice
1 to 1½ cups EQUAL® SPOONFUL*

*May substitute 24 to 36 packets Equal® sweetener.

• Coarsely mash peaches in large bowl with potato masher or pastry blender (about 2½ cups).

• Gradually stir pectin into apple juice in medium saucepan. Heat mixture to a rolling boil (one that does not stop when being stirred) over high heat, stirring constantly; boil, stirring constantly, 1 minute.

• Stir hot mixture into peaches; stir in Equal®. Fill jars, allowing ½ inch headspace. Cool jam; seal and freeze up to 3 months.

Makes 3 (½-pint) jars

Nutrients per Serving (1 tablespoon):	
Calories:	16
Fat:	0 g
Protein:	0 g
Carbohydrate:	4 g
Cholesterol:	0 mg
Sodium:	2 mg

Dietary Exchanges: Free Food

Irish Cream Iced Cappuccino

43% calorie reduction from traditional recipe

¹⁄₂ **cup cocoa**
¹⁄₂ **cup instant coffee granules**
 1 **cup water**
¹⁄₂ **cup EQUAL® SPOONFUL***
 6 **cups fat-free milk**
¹⁄₂ **cup liquid Irish cream coffee creamer**

*May substitute 12 packets Equal® sweetener.

• Whisk together first 3 ingredients in large saucepan until smooth. Bring to a boil over medium heat, whisking constantly; boil, whisking constantly, 2 minutes. Remove mixture from heat; add Equal®. Cool slightly.

• Whisk in milk and creamer. Cover and chill at least 4 hours or up to 2 days.

• Serve over ice. *Makes 8 servings*

Nutrients per Serving:	
Calories:	123
Fat:	2 g
Protein:	9 g
Carbohydrate:	18 g
Cholesterol:	4 mg
Sodium:	102 mg

Dietary Exchanges: 1½ Milk

Triple-Berry Jam

80% calorie reduction from traditional recipe

> 4 cups fresh strawberries or thawed frozen unsweetened strawberries
> 2 cups fresh raspberries or thawed frozen unsweetened raspberries
> 1 cup fresh blueberries or thawed frozen unsweetened blueberries
> 1 package (1¾ ounces) no-sugar-needed pectin
> ¾ cup EQUAL® SPOONFUL*

May substitute 18 packets Equal® sweetener.

• Mash strawberries, raspberries and blueberries by hand or with food processor to make 4 cups pulp. Stir in pectin; let mixture stand 10 minutes, stirring frequently.

• Transfer to large saucepan. Cook and stir over medium heat until mixture comes to a boil. Cook and stir 1 minute more. Remove from heat; stir in Equal®. Skim off foam, if necessary.

• Immediately fill containers, leaving ½ inch headspace. Seal and let stand at room temperature until firm (several hours). Store up to 2 weeks in refrigerator or 3 months in freezer.

Makes 8 (½-pint) jars

Nutrients per Serving (1 tablespoon):	
Calories:	9
Fat:	0 g
Protein:	0 g
Carbohydrate:	2 g
Cholesterol:	0 mg
Sodium:	3 mg

Dietary Exchanges: Free Food

Coffee Latte

61% calorie reduction from traditional recipe

1¼ cups regular grind espresso or other dark roast coffee
1 cinnamon stick, broken into pieces
6 cups water
⅓ cup EQUAL® SPOONFUL*
2½ cups fat-free milk
Ground cinnamon or nutmeg

*May substitute 8 packets Equal® sweetener.

• Place espresso and cinnamon stick in filter basket of drip coffee pot; brew coffee with water. Stir Equal® into coffee; pour into 8 mugs or cups.

• Heat milk in small saucepan until steaming. Blend half of milk in blender at high speed about 15 seconds until foamy; pour milk into 4 mugs of coffee, spooning foam on top. Repeat with remaining milk and coffee. Sprinkle with cinnamon or nutmeg before serving.   *Makes 8 (8-ounce) servings*

Nutrients per Serving:	
Calories:	31
Fat:	0g
Protein:	3g
Carbohydrate:	5g
Cholesterol:	1mg
Sodium:	46mg

Dietary Exchanges: ½ Milk

Cinnamon Equal®

88% calorie reduction from traditional recipe

½ cup EQUAL® SPOONFUL*
½ teaspoon ground cinnamon

*May substitute 12 packets Equal® sweetener.

• Combine Equal® and cinnamon in a shaker jar or bowl.

• Sprinkling ideas: toast, French toast, cereal, fresh fruit, applesauce, yogurt, cottage cheese, hot cocoa and coffee, warm fruit pies and cobblers.   *Makes 24 servings*

Nutrients per Serving *(1 teaspoon)*:

Calories:	2
Fat:	0g
Protein:	0g
Carbohydrate:	0g
Cholesterol:	0mg
Sodium:	0mg

Dietary Exchanges: Free Food

Lemonade

81% calorie reduction from traditional recipe

> **1 cup fresh lemon juice or frozen lemon juice concentrate***
> **¾ cup EQUAL® SPOONFUL****
> **4 cups cold water**
> **Ice cubes**

such as Minute Maid® Premium Lemon Juice (frozen) 100% Pure Lemon Juice from Concentrate

**May substitute 18 packets Equal® sweetener.*

• Combine lemon juice and Equal® in large pitcher; stir to dissolve Equal®. Add water; blend well.

• Serve over ice.   *Makes 6 servings*

Nutrients per Serving:

Calories:	20
Fat:	0g
Protein:	0g
Carbohydrate:	6g
Cholesterol:	0mg
Sodium:	6mg

Dietary Exchanges: ½ Fruit

Strawberry Limeade

80% calorie reduction from traditional recipe

1½ cups quartered fresh strawberries
1 cup fresh or bottled lime juice
4 cups water
1½ cups EQUAL® SPOONFUL*
6 small whole strawberries or lime wedges (optional)

*May substitute 36 packets Equal® sweetener.

• Blend strawberries and lime juice in blender or food processor until smooth. Combine strawberry mixture, water and Equal® in pitcher.

• Pour over ice cubes in tall glasses; garnish each with strawberry or lime wedge, if desired. *Makes 6 servings*

Nutrients per Serving:	
Calories:	43
Fat:	0g
Protein:	0g
Carbohydrate:	11g
Cholesterol:	0mg
Sodium:	6mg

Dietary Exchanges: 1 Fruit

Entrées, Salads & Sides

Cucumber Tomato Salad

45% calorie reduction from traditional recipe

> ½ cup rice vinegar*
> 3 tablespoons EQUAL® SPOONFUL**
> 3 cups unpeeled ¼-inch-thick sliced cucumbers, quartered (about 2 medium)
> 2 cups chopped tomato (about 1 large)
> ½ cup chopped red onion
> Salt and pepper to taste

Distilled white vinegar may be substituted for rice vinegar.

**May substitute 4½ packets Equal® sweetener.*

• Combine vinegar and Equal®. Add cucumbers, tomato and onion. Season to taste with salt and pepper; mix well. Refrigerate, covered, at least 30 minutes before serving.

Makes 6 servings

Nutrients per Serving:	
Calories:	22
Fat:	0 g
Protein:	1 g
Carbohydrate:	5 g
Cholesterol:	0 mg
Sodium:	7 mg

Dietary Exchanges: 1 Vegetable

Cranberry Salad

56% calorie reduction from traditional recipe

> 2 cups cranberries
> 1 cup water
> 1 cup EQUAL® SPOONFUL*
> 1 small package cranberry or cherry sugar-free gelatin
> 1 cup boiling water
> 1 cup diced celery
> 1 can (7¼ ounces) crushed pineapple, in juice
> ½ cup chopped walnuts

*May substitute 24 packets Equal® sweetener.

• Bring cranberries and 1 cup water to a boil. Remove from heat when cranberries have popped open. Add Equal® and stir. Set aside to cool.

• Dissolve gelatin with 1 cup boiling water. Add cranberry sauce; mix thoroughly. Add celery, pineapple and walnuts. Pour into mold or bowl. Place in refrigerator until set.

Makes 8 servings

Nutrients per Serving:	
Calories:	92
Fat:	5 g
Protein:	2 g
Carbohydrate:	9 g
Cholesterol:	0 mg
Sodium:	43 mg

Dietary Exchanges: 1 Fruit, 1 Fat

Gingered Chicken with Vegetables

26% calorie reduction from traditional recipe

>   2 tablespoons vegetable oil, divided
>   1 pound boneless skinless chicken breasts, cut into
>   thin strips
>   1 cup red bell pepper strips
>   1 cup sliced fresh mushrooms
>   16 fresh pea pods, cut in half crosswise
>   ½ cup sliced water chestnuts
>   ¼ cup sliced green onions
>   1 tablespoon grated fresh gingerroot
>   1 large clove garlic, crushed
>   ⅔ cup reduced-fat, reduced-sodium chicken broth
>   2 tablespoons EQUAL® SPOONFUL*
>   2 tablespoons light soy sauce
>   4 teaspoons cornstarch
>   2 teaspoons dark sesame oil
>   Salt and pepper to taste

*May substitute 3 packets Equal® sweetener.

• Heat 1 tablespoon vegetable oil in large skillet over medium-high heat. Stir-fry chicken until no longer pink; remove chicken from skillet. Heat remaining 1 tablespoon vegetable oil in skillet. Add bell peppers, mushrooms, pea pods, water chestnuts, green onions, ginger and garlic to skillet. Stir-fry mixture 3 to 4 minutes until vegetables are crisp-tender.

• Meanwhile, combine chicken broth, Equal®, soy sauce, cornstarch and sesame oil until smooth. Stir into skillet mixture. Cook over medium heat until thick and clear. Stir in chicken; heat through. Season with salt and pepper to taste. Serve over hot cooked rice, if desired.   *Makes 4 servings*

Nutrients per Serving:	
Calories:	263
Fat:	11 g
Protein:	29 g
Carbohydrate:	11 g
Cholesterol:	66 mg
Sodium:	411 mg

Dietary Exchanges: 2 Vegetable, 4 Lean Meat

Marinated Carrot Salad

28% calorie reduction from traditional recipe

2 pounds carrots, sliced, or small carrots
1 can (10¾ ounces) tomato soup
1 cup EQUAL® SPOONFUL*
1 medium onion, chopped
1 green bell pepper, chopped
¾ cup wine vinegar
½ cup vegetable oil or olive oil
1 teaspoon Worcestershire sauce
1 teaspoon salt
1 teaspoon ground black pepper
1 teaspoon Dijon mustard

*May substitute 24 packets Equal® sweetener.

• Boil carrots until tender; drain.

• Combine remaining ingredients in small bowl. Pour over carrots; mix well.

• Refrigerate in covered container at least 12 hours.

Makes 12 servings

Nutrients per Serving:	
Calories:	151
Fat:	10g
Protein:	2g
Carbohydrate:	16g
Cholesterol:	0mg
Sodium:	399mg

Dietary Exchanges: 3 Vegetable, 2 Fat

Ham with Cherry Sauce

23% calorie reduction from traditional recipe

> **5 pound fully cooked boneless ham**
> **Whole cloves**

Cherry Sauce
> **2 cans (16 ounces each) red tart pitted cherries in juice,**
> **undrained (see Tip)**
> **⅔ to ¾ cup unsweetened pineapple juice**
> **4 teaspoons lemon juice**
> **¼ cup cornstarch**
> **1 to 1½ cups EQUAL® SPOONFUL***
> **Red food coloring (optional)**

*May substitute 24 to 36 packets Equal® sweetener.

• Place ham in roasting pan; stud with cloves. Roast ham in preheated 325°F oven about 1½ hours or until thermometer inserted in center of ham registers 160°F.

• For Cherry Sauce, drain cherries, reserving juice in 2-cup glass measure. Add enough pineapple juice to make 2 cups. Pour juice mixture and lemon juice into medium saucepan; whisk in cornstarch until smooth.

• Heat to a boil, whisking constantly, about 1 minute. Add cherries to saucepan; cook over medium heat 3 to 4 minutes or until heated through. Stir in Equal® and food coloring.

• Slice ham and arrange on platter with bowl of Cherry Sauce in center. Garnish with parsley.   *Makes 16 servings*

Tip: 2 packages (16 ounces each) frozen no-sugar-added pitted cherries, thawed, can be substituted for the canned cherries; drain cherries thoroughly and add enough pineapple juice to make 2 cups. Proceed with recipe as directed above.

Nutrients per Serving:	
Calories:	246
Fat:	8g
Protein:	30g
Carbohydrate:	12g
Cholesterol:	75mg
Sodium:	1710mg

Dietary Exchanges: 1 Fruit, 4 Lean Meat

Tangy Apple Slaw

44% calorie reduction from traditional recipe

> 4 cups shredded green cabbage
> 1 cup shredded carrots
> 1 cup chopped unpeeled apple (1 medium)
> ½ cup thinly sliced red or green bell pepper strips
> ⅔ cup light mayonnaise or salad dressing
> ⅓ cup reduced-fat sour cream
> 3 tablespoons EQUAL® SPOONFUL*
> 1½ tablespoons Dijon mustard
> 1 tablespoon lemon juice
> ⅛ teaspoon pepper

*May substitute 4½ packets Equal® sweetener.

• Combine cabbage, carrots, apple and bell pepper in medium size bowl. Mix mayonnaise, sour cream, Equal®, mustard, lemon juice and pepper in small bowl; stir until well blended. Spoon Equal® mixture over cabbage mixture; gently toss to combine. Refrigerate, covered, 1 to 2 hours to allow flavors to blend.

Makes 6 servings

Nutrients per Serving:	
Calories:	152
Fat:	11 g
Protein:	2 g
Carbohydrate:	13 g
Cholesterol:	15 mg
Sodium:	331 mg

Dietary Exchanges: 2 Vegetable, 2 Fat

Southern Style Mustard BBQ Chicken Kabobs

31% calorie reduction from traditional recipe

> 1½ cups catsup
> 1 cup prepared mustard
> ½ to ⅔ cup cider vinegar
> ½ cup EQUAL® SPOONFUL*
> 2 tablespoons stick butter or margarine
> 1 tablespoon Worcestershire sauce
> ½ teaspoon maple flavoring
> ½ teaspoon coarsely ground black pepper
> 1½ pounds skinless, boneless chicken breasts, cut into ¾-inch cubes
> 2 small yellow squash, cut crosswise into 1-inch slices
> 12 medium mushroom caps
> 1 large red or green bell pepper, cut into 1-inch pieces

May substitute 12 packets Equal® sweetener.

• Mix all ingredients, except chicken and vegetables, in medium saucepan. Cook over medium heat 3 to 4 minutes or until sauce is hot and butter is melted.

• Assemble chicken cubes and vegetables on skewers; grill over medium heat 10 to 15 minutes until chicken is no longer pink, turning occasionally and basting generously with sauce. Heat remaining sauce and serve with kabobs.   *Makes 6 servings*

Tip: Kabobs can also be broiled. Broil 6 inches from heat source until chicken is no longer pink and vegetables are tender, 10 to 12 minutes, turning occasionally and basting with sauce.

Nutrients per Serving:	
Calories:	285
Fat:	8 g
Protein:	30 g
Carbohydrate:	27 g
Cholesterol:	66 mg
Sodium:	1397 mg

Dietary Exchanges: 1½ Starch, 1 Vegetable, 3 Lean Meat

Reunion Salad

52% calorie reduction from traditional recipe

1 large head broccoli
1 small red onion, halved and thinly sliced
½ cup raisins
⅓ cup chopped pecans or sunflower seeds
¾ cup light salad dressing or mayonnaise
½ cup EQUAL® SPOONFUL*
2 tablespoons fat-free milk
2 tablespoons white vinegar
    Salt and pepper to taste
4 slices bacon, cooked crisp and crumbled

*May substitute 12 packets Equal® sweetener.

• Clean, trim and chop broccoli into large bowl. Add onion, raisins and pecans.

• Mix together salad dressing, Equal®, milk and vinegar, stirring until smooth. Pour dressing over salad; add salt and pepper to taste. Cover and refrigerate overnight.

• Top with bacon bits before serving.   *Makes 8 servings*

Nutrients per Serving:	
Calories:	217
Fat:	14g
Protein:	5g
Carbohydrate:	21g
Cholesterol:	13mg
Sodium:	259mg

Dietary Exchanges: ½ Fruit, 3 Vegetable, 3 Fat

Citrus Bean Salad

32% calorie reduction from traditional recipe

>   3 naval oranges, peeled, sliced, membranes removed
> 1½ cups finely shredded carrots
>   1 can (15½ ounces) red kidney beans, rinsed and drained
>   1 can (15½ ounces) Great Northern beans, rinsed and drained
>   ⅓ cup chopped fresh parsley
>   ⅓ cup chopped green bell pepper
>   ⅓ cup tarragon white wine vinegar
>   ¼ cup balsamic vinegar
>   ¼ cup EQUAL® SPOONFUL*
>   Salt and pepper to taste
>   12 lettuce leaves

May substitute 6 packets Equal® sweetener.

• Combine oranges, carrots, kidney beans and Great Northern beans in large non-metallic bowl. Cover and chill.

• Combine parsley, bell pepper, vinegar and Equal® in medium bowl and stir well. Cover and refrigerate dressing until chilled.

• Pour dressing over orange-vegetable mixture; add salt and pepper to taste. Let stand to blend flavors. Keep refrigerated until ready to serve.

• Serve over lettuce leaves on individual plates.

Makes 6 servings

Nutrients per Serving:	
Calories:	231
Fat:	1 g
Protein:	12 g
Carbohydrate:	47 g
Cholesterol:	0 mg
Sodium:	19 mg

Dietary Exchanges: 2 Starch, ½ Fruit, 1½ Vegetable

Sweet and Sour Carrots

26% calorie reduction from traditional recipe

2 cups carrot slices, ¼ inch thick
½ cup celery slices, ½ inch thick
1 can (8 ounces) pineapple tidbits (drain and reserve juice)
1 tablespoon vinegar
2 teaspoons cornstarch
1 teaspoon light soy sauce
⅛ teaspoon salt
2 tablespoons stick butter or margarine
¼ cup sliced green onions
¼ cup EQUAL® SPOONFUL*

*May substitute 6 packets Equal® sweetener.

• Cook carrots and celery in medium saucepan in small amount of water about 8 minutes or until tender. Drain and set aside.

• Add enough water to reserved pineapple juice to make ½ cup liquid. Stir in vinegar, cornstarch, soy sauce and salt. Cook in medium saucepan until liquid thickens.

• Add butter, drained pineapple and green onions; cook and stir until heated through. Add drained carrots and celery; cook about 2 minutes or until heated through. Stir in Equal®.

Makes 6 servings

Nutrients per Serving:	
Calories:	80
Fat:	4 g
Protein:	1 g
Carbohydrate:	11 g
Cholesterol:	0 mg
Sodium:	170 mg

Dietary Exchanges: 2 Vegetable, 1 Fat

Thai Broccoli Salad

36% calorie reduction from traditional recipe

¼ cup creamy or chunky peanut butter
2 tablespoons EQUAL® SPOONFUL*
1½ tablespoons hot water
1 tablespoon lime juice
1 tablespoon light soy sauce
1½ teaspoons dark sesame oil
¼ teaspoon red pepper flakes
2 tablespoons vegetable oil
3 cups fresh broccoli florets
½ cup chopped red bell pepper
¼ cup sliced green onions
1 clove garlic, crushed

*May substitute 3 packets Equal® sweetener.

• Combine peanut butter, Equal®, hot water, lime juice, soy sauce, sesame oil and red pepper flakes until well blended; set aside.

• Heat vegetable oil in large skillet over medium-high heat. Add broccoli, bell pepper, green onions and garlic. Stir-fry 3 to 4 minutes until vegetables are tender-crisp. Remove from heat and stir in peanut butter mixture.

• Serve warm or at room temperature.   *Makes 4 servings*

Nutrients per Serving:	
Calories:	199
Fat:	17 g
Protein:	6 g
Carbohydrate:	9 g
Cholesterol:	0 mg
Sodium:	342 mg

Dietary Exchanges: 2 Vegetable, 3 Fat

Cookies & Bars

Chocolate Chip Cookies

28% calorie reduction from traditional recipe

⅓ **cup stick butter or margarine, softened**
1 **egg**
1 **teaspoon vanilla**
⅓ **cup EQUAL® SPOONFUL***
⅓ **cup firmly packed light brown sugar**
¾ **cup all-purpose flour**
½ **teaspoon baking soda**
¼ **teaspoon salt**
½ **cup semi-sweet chocolate chips or mini chocolate chips**

*May substitute 8 packets Equal® sweetener.

• Beat butter with electric mixer until fluffy. Beat in egg and vanilla until blended. Mix in Equal® and brown sugar until combined.

• Combine flour, baking soda and salt. Mix into butter mixture until well blended. Stir in chocolate chips.

• Drop dough by rounded teaspoonfuls onto ungreased baking sheet. Bake in preheated 350°F oven 8 to 10 minutes or until light golden color. Remove from baking sheet and cool completely on wire rack.   *Makes about 2 dozen cookies*

Nutrients per Serving *(1 cookie)*:	
Calories:	67
Fat:	4g
Protein:	1g
Carbohydrate:	8g
Cholesterol:	16mg
Sodium:	80mg
Dietary Exchanges: ½ Starch, 1 Fat	

Double Chocolate Brownies

33% calorie reduction from traditional recipe

> ¾ cup all-purpose flour
> 1 cup EQUAL® SPOONFUL*
> ½ cup semi-sweet chocolate chips or mini chocolate chips
> 6 tablespoons unsweetened cocoa
> 1 teaspoon baking powder
> ¼ teaspoon salt
> 6 tablespoons stick butter or margarine, softened
> ½ cup unsweetened applesauce
> 2 eggs
> 1 teaspoon vanilla

*May substitute 24 packets Equal® sweetener.

• Combine flour, Equal®, chocolate chips, cocoa, baking powder and salt. Beat butter, applesauce, eggs and vanilla until blended. Stir in combined flour mixture until blended.

• Spread batter in 8-inch square baking pan sprayed with nonstick cooking spray. Bake in preheated 350°F oven 18 to 20 minutes or until top springs back when gently touched. Cool completely on wire rack.   *Makes 16 servings*

Nutrients per Serving:	
Calories:	108
Fat:	7g
Protein:	2g
Carbohydrate:	10g
Cholesterol:	38mg
Sodium:	119mg

Dietary Exchanges: 1 Starch, 1 Fat

Orange Cranberry Cookies

20% calorie reduction from traditional recipe

¼ cup stick butter or margarine
1 egg
3 tablespoons frozen orange juice concentrate
¾ cup all-purpose flour, sifted
⅓ cup EQUAL® SPOONFUL*
¼ cup quick oats, uncooked
1 teaspoon grated orange peel
¼ teaspoon baking soda
⅛ teaspoon cream of tartar
   Dash salt
½ cup dried cranberries
½ cup chopped walnuts

May substitute 8 packets Equal® sweetener.

• Beat butter in medium bowl. Beat in egg and frozen orange juice concentrate.

• Combine flour, Equal®, oats, orange peel, baking soda, cream of tartar and salt in separate bowl.

• Add flour mixture to creamed mixture and mix well. Stir in cranberries and walnuts.

• Drop by rounded teaspoonfuls onto ungreased baking sheet.

• Bake in preheated 375°F oven 8 to 10 minutes or until bottoms are lightly browned. Remove from baking sheet and cool completely on wire rack.   *Makes 24 cookies*

Nutrients per Serving *(1 cookie)*:	
Calories:	66
Fat:	4g
Protein:	1g
Carbohydrate:	7g
Cholesterol:	9mg
Sodium:	38mg

Dietary Exchanges: ½ Starch, ½ Fat

Peanut Butter Chocolate Bars

21% calorie reduction from traditional recipe

> 1 cup EQUAL® SPOONFUL*
> ½ cup stick butter or margarine, softened
> ⅓ cup firmly packed brown sugar
> ½ cup 2% milk
> ½ cup creamy peanut butter
> 1 egg
> 1 teaspoon vanilla
> 1 cup all-purpose flour
> 1 cup quick oats, uncooked
> ½ teaspoon baking soda
> ¼ teaspoon salt
> ¾ cup mini semi-sweet chocolate chips

*May substitute 24 packets Equal® sweetener.

• Beat Equal®, butter and brown sugar until well combined. Stir in milk, peanut butter, egg and vanilla until blended. Gradually mix in combined flour, oats, baking soda and salt until blended. Stir in chocolate chips.

• Spread mixture evenly in 13×9-inch baking pan generously coated with nonstick cooking spray. Bake in preheated 350°F oven 20 to 22 minutes. Cool completely in pan on wire rack. Cut into squares; store in airtight container at room temperature.

Makes 48 bars

Nutrients per Serving *(1 bar):*	
Calories:	75
Fat:	5 g
Protein:	1 g
Carbohydrate:	8 g
Cholesterol:	10 mg
Sodium:	60 mg

Dietary Exchanges: ½ Starch, 1 Fat

Apple Raisin Oatmeal Cookies

30% calorie reduction from traditional recipe

1¼ cups EQUAL® SPOONFUL*
1 cup unsweetened applesauce**
½ cup firmly packed brown sugar
6 tablespoons stick butter or margarine, softened
⅓ cup 2% milk
1 egg
2 teaspoons vanilla
2 cups all-purpose flour
1 teaspoon baking soda
1 teaspoon ground cinnamon
¼ teaspoon ground nutmeg
¼ teaspoon salt
1½ cups quick oats, uncooked
1 cup raisins

May substitute 30 packets Equal® sweetener.

**Apple butter may be substituted for the unsweetened applesauce.*

• Combine Equal®, applesauce, brown sugar, butter, milk, egg and vanilla. Mix with electric mixer until well blended. Stir in combined flour, baking soda, cinnamon, nutmeg and salt. Gradually mix in oats and raisins until well combined.

• Drop by tablespoonfuls onto baking sheets lightly sprayed with nonstick cooking spray. Bake in preheated 350°F oven 10 to 12 minutes. Remove from baking sheets and cool completely on wire racks. *Makes about 4 dozen cookies*

Nutrients per Serving *(1 cookie)*:	
Calories:	64
Fat:	2g
Protein:	1g
Carbohydrate:	11g
Cholesterol:	8mg
Sodium:	57mg

Dietary Exchanges: 1 Starch

Special Crunchy Cookies

25% calorie reduction from traditional recipe

> 1 cup EQUAL® SPOONFUL*
> ½ cup stick butter or margarine, softened
> 1 egg
> 1 teaspoon vanilla
> 4 cups Kellogg's® Special K® cereal, crushed to 1½ cups, divided
> 1 cup all-purpose flour
> 1 teaspoon baking powder
> ¼ teaspoon salt
> ½ cup mini semi-sweet chocolate chips

*May substitute 24 packets Equal® sweetener.

• Beat Equal® and butter on medium speed of electric mixer until light and fluffy. Beat in egg and vanilla until well combined.

• Stir in combined 1 cup crushed cereal, flour, baking powder and salt until well blended. Stir in chocolate chips. Shape dough into balls using rounded measuring teaspoons. Roll in remaining ½ cup crushed cereal. Place on ungreased baking sheet.

• Bake in preheated 375°F oven 8 to 10 minutes. Remove from baking sheet and cool completely on wire rack.

Makes about 4 dozen cookies

Nutrients per Serving *(2 cookies):*	
Calories:	92
Fat:	6g
Protein:	2g
Carbohydrate:	10g
Cholesterol:	20mg
Sodium:	128mg

Dietary Exchanges: ½ Starch, 1 Fat

Pumpkin Polka Dot Cookies

19% calorie reduction from traditional recipe

1¼ cups EQUAL® SPOONFUL*
½ cup stick butter or margarine, softened
3 tablespoons light molasses
1 cup canned pumpkin
1 egg
1½ teaspoons vanilla
1⅔ cups all-purpose flour
1 teaspoon baking powder
1¼ teaspoons ground cinnamon
½ teaspoon ground nutmeg
½ teaspoon ground ginger
½ teaspoon baking soda
¼ teaspoon salt
1 cup mini semi-sweet chocolate chips

*May substitute 30 packets Equal® sweetener.

• Beat Equal®, butter and molasses until well combined. Mix in pumpkin, egg and vanilla until blended. Gradually stir in combined flour, baking powder, spices, baking soda and salt until well blended. Stir in chocolate chips.

• Drop by teaspoonfuls onto baking sheet coated with nonstick cooking spray. Bake in preheated 350°F oven 11 to 13 minutes. Remove from baking sheet and cool completely on wire rack. Store at room temperature in airtight container up to 1 week.

Makes about 4 dozen cookies

Nutrients per Serving (1 cookie):	
Calories:	63
Fat:	3g
Protein:	1g
Carbohydrate:	8g
Cholesterol:	10mg
Sodium:	69mg

Dietary Exchanges: ½ Starch, ½ Fat

Pies & Tarts

Blueberry Pie

30% calorie reduction from traditional recipe

> 6 cups fresh or 2 packages (16 ounces each) frozen
>   unsweetened blueberries
> 3 tablespoons lemon juice
> 1 cup plus 2 tablespoons EQUAL® SPOONFUL*
> 6 tablespoons cornstarch
>   Pastry for double-crust 9-inch pie

*May substitute 27 packets Equal® sweetener.

• Toss blueberries and lemon juice in large bowl. Sprinkle with combined Equal® and cornstarch; toss to coat. (If frozen blueberries are used, let stand 30 minutes.)

• Roll half of pastry on lightly floured surface into circle 1 inch larger than inverted 9-inch pie pan. Ease pastry into pan; trim within 1 inch of edge of pan. Roll remaining pastry to ⅛-inch thickness; cut into 10 to 12 strips, ½ inch wide.

• Pour blueberry mixture into pastry. Arrange pastry strips over filling and weave into lattice design. Trim ends of lattice strips; fold edge of lower crust over ends of lattice strips. Seal and flute edge.

• Bake in preheated 400°F oven 55 to 60 minutes or until pastry is browned and filling is bubbly. Cover edge of crust with aluminum foil if browning too quickly. Cool on wire rack; refrigerate leftovers.   *Makes 8 servings*

Nutrients per Serving:	
Calories:	257
Fat:	10g
Protein:	3g
Carbohydrate:	42g
Cholesterol:	10mg
Sodium:	128mg

Dietary Exchanges: 1½ Starch, 1½ Fruit, 2 Fat

Sweet Potato Pie

33% calorie reduction from traditional recipe

Pastry for single-crust 9-inch pie
2 cups cooked, mashed sweet potatoes (about 2 pounds)
1 can (12 ounces) evaporated fat-free milk
1 cup EQUAL® SPOONFUL*
2 eggs, lightly beaten
1 tablespoon all-purpose flour
1 teaspoon lemon juice
1 teaspoon vanilla
½ teaspoon ground cinnamon
½ teaspoon ground nutmeg
½ teaspoon salt

*May substitute 24 packets Equal® sweetener.

• Roll pastry on lightly floured surface into circle 1 inch larger than inverted 9-inch pie pan. Ease pastry into pan; trim and flute edge.

• Mix sweet potatoes with electric mixer in large bowl until smooth. Stir in evaporated milk, Equal®, eggs, flour, lemon juice, vanilla, spices and salt. Pour mixture into pastry shell.

• Bake in preheated 400°F oven 40 to 45 minutes or until filling is set and sharp knife inserted near center comes out clean.

• Cool completely on wire rack. Refrigerate until serving time.

Makes 8 servings

Nutrients per Serving:	
Calories:	234
Fat:	8 g
Protein:	7 g
Carbohydrate:	32 g
Cholesterol:	62 mg
Sodium:	326 mg

Dietary Exchanges: 2 Starch, 1½ Fat

Country Peach Tart

18% calorie reduction from traditional recipe

Pastry for single-crust 9-inch pie
4 cups sliced pitted peeled fresh peaches or frozen peaches,
thawed
½ cup EQUAL® SPOONFUL*
1 tablespoon all-purpose flour
½ teaspoon ground cinnamon
¼ teaspoon almond extract

*May substitute 12 packets Equal® sweetener.

• Roll pastry on lightly floured surface to 12-inch circle; transfer to ungreased baking sheet. Combine peaches, Equal®, flour, cinnamon and almond extract; toss gently until peaches are evenly coated with mixture.

• Arrange peach mixture over pastry, leaving 2-inch border around edge of pastry. Bring edge of pastry toward center, overlapping as necessary.

• Bake tart in preheated 425°F oven 25 to 30 minutes or until crust is golden brown and peaches are tender. Serve warm or at room temperature.   *Makes 8 servings*

Nutrients per Serving:	
Calories:	161
Fat:	7 g
Protein:	2 g
Carbohydrate:	23 g
Cholesterol:	5 mg
Sodium:	100 mg

Dietary Exchanges: 1 Starch, ½ Fruit, 1 Fat

Nectarine and Berry Pie

31% calorie reduction from traditional recipe

> **Pastry for single-crust 9-inch pie**
> 5 **cups sliced nectarines**
> 1 **cup raspberries or sliced strawberries**
> 1 **cup fresh or frozen blueberries, partially thawed**
> 2 **teaspoons lemon juice**
> 1 **cup EQUAL® SPOONFUL***
> 3 **tablespoons cornstarch**
> 1 **teaspoon grated lemon peel**
> ¼ **teaspoon ground allspice**

*May substitute 24 packets Equal® sweetener.

• Roll pastry on floured surface into 12-inch circle; transfer to ungreased baking sheet.

• Toss nectarines and berries with lemon juice in large bowl; sprinkle fruit with combined Equal®, cornstarch, lemon peel and allspice and toss to coat. Arrange fruit over pastry, leaving 2-inch border around edge of pastry. Bring edge of pastry toward center, overlapping as necessary.

• Bake pie in preheated 425°F oven 35 to 40 minutes or until pastry is golden and fruit is tender. Cool on wire rack.

Makes 8 servings

Nutrients per Serving:	
Calories:	172
Fat:	7 g
Protein:	2 g
Carbohydrate:	31 g
Cholesterol:	5 mg
Sodium:	64 mg

Dietary Exchanges: 1 Starch, 1 Fruit, 1 Fat

Apple Streusel Pie

29% calorie reduction from traditional recipe

Pastry for single-crust 9-inch pie
¾ cup EQUAL® SPOONFUL*
2 tablespoons cornstarch
2 tablespoons lemon juice
¾ teaspoon ground cinnamon
¼ teaspoon salt
⅛ teaspoon ground nutmeg
6 cups sliced, cored, peeled Granny Smith apples (about 6)
½ cup all-purpose flour
½ cup EQUAL® SPOONFUL**
½ teaspoon ground cinnamon
¼ teaspoon salt
4 tablespoons stick butter or margarine, melted
½ cup chopped nuts

*May substitute 18 packets Equal® sweetener.

**May substitute 12 packets Equal® sweetener.

• Roll pastry on floured surface into circle 1 inch larger than inverted 9-inch pie pan. Ease pastry into pan; trim and flute edge.

• Combine ¾ cup Equal® Spoonful, cornstarch, lemon juice, ¾ teaspoon cinnamon, ¼ teaspoon salt and nutmeg. Sprinkle over apples in large bowl and toss. Spoon apples into pie crust.

• Combine flour, ½ cup Equal® Spoonful, ½ teaspoon cinnamon and ¼ teaspoon salt. Stir in butter until mixture resembles coarse crumbs. Stir in nuts. Sprinkle over apples. Bake in preheated 375°F oven 45 to 55 minutes or until apples are tender and crust is golden. Cool on wire rack. *Makes 8 servings*

Nutrients per Serving:	
Calories:	269
Fat:	11g
Protein:	2g
Carbohydrate:	26g
Cholesterol:	16mg
Sodium:	158mg

Dietary Exchanges: 1 Starch, 1 Fruit, 2 Fat

Lemon Meringue Pie

48% calorie reduction from traditional recipe

Pastry for single-crust 9-inch pie
2¼ **cups water**
½ **cup fresh lemon juice or frozen lemon juice concentrate***
½ **cup cornstarch**
2 **eggs**
2 **egg whites**
1½ **teaspoons grated lemon peel**
1½ **cups EQUAL® SPOONFUL****
2 **tablespoons stick butter or margarine**
1 **to 2 drops yellow food coloring (optional)**
3 **egg whites**
¼ **teaspoon cream of tartar**
⅔ **cup EQUAL® SPOONFUL*****

**such as Minute Maid® Premium Lemon Juice (frozen) 100% Pure Lemon
Juice from Concentrate*

**May substitute 36 packets Equal® sweetener.

***May substitute 16 packets Equal® sweetener.

• Roll pastry on lightly floured surface into circle 1 inch larger
than inverted 9-inch pie pan. Ease pastry into pan; trim and
flute edge. Pierce bottom and side of pastry with fork. Bake in
preheated 425°F oven 10 to 12 minutes or until pastry is golden.
Cool on wire rack.

• Combine water, lemon juice and cornstarch in medium
saucepan. Bring to a boil over medium-high heat, stirring
constantly; boil and stir 1 minute. Beat eggs, 2 egg whites and
lemon peel in medium bowl. Mix in 1½ cups Equal® Spoonful.
Stir about half of hot cornstarch mixture into egg mixture.

• Return all to saucepan. Cook and stir over low heat 1 minute.
Remove from heat; stir in butter until melted. Stir in food
coloring, if desired. Pour mixture into baked pie shell.

continued on page 62

Lemon Meringue Pie, continued

• Beat 3 egg whites in medium bowl until foamy. Add cream of tartar and beat to soft peaks. Gradually beat in ⅔ cup Equal® Spoonful, beating to stiff peaks. Spread meringue over hot lemon filling, carefully sealing to edge of crust to prevent shrinking or weeping.

• Bake pie in 425°F oven about 5 minutes or until meringue is lightly browned.

• Cool completely on wire rack before cutting.

Makes 8 servings

Nutrients per Serving:

Calories:	189
Fat:	10 g
Protein:	5 g
Carbohydrate:	19 g
Cholesterol:	61 mg
Sodium:	228 mg

Dietary Exchanges: 1 Starch, 2 Fat

Tip:

One medium-size lemon will yield about 3 to 4 tablespoons of juice. You'll find that thin-skinned lemons usually yield more juice, but it is easier to remove the zest and the peel of thick-skinned ones. Room-temperature lemons also yield more juice than cold ones. To get as much juice as possible from a lemon, roll it around on the counter under the flat of your hand before cutting it in half. This releases juice from the small sacs of the lemon.

Pumpkin Pie

31% calorie reduction from traditional recipe

Pastry for single-crust 9-inch pie
1 **can (16 ounces) pumpkin**
1 **can (12 ounces) evaporated fat-free milk**
3 **eggs**
¾ **cup EQUAL® SPOONFUL***
1 **teaspoon vanilla**
1 **teaspoon ground cinnamon**
¼ **teaspoon ground ginger**
¼ **teaspoon ground nutmeg**
¼ **teaspoon salt**

*May substitute 18 packets Equal® sweetener.

• Roll pastry on floured surface into circle 1 inch larger than inverted 9-inch pie pan. Ease pastry into pan; trim and flute edge.

• Beat pumpkin, evaporated milk and eggs in medium bowl; beat in remaining ingredients. Pour into pastry shell. Bake in preheated 400°F oven 35 to 40 minutes or until knife inserted into center comes out clean.

• Cool on wire rack.   *Makes 8 servings*

Nutrients per Serving:	
Calories:	175
Fat:	7g
Protein:	8g
Carbohydrate:	22g
Cholesterol:	86mg
Sodium:	208mg

Dietary Exchanges: 1 Starch, ½ Milk, 1 Fat

Fresh Strawberry Cream Pie

24% calorie reduction from traditional recipe

1 quart fresh medium strawberries
1 tablespoon EQUAL® SPOONFUL*
Pastry for single-crust 9-inch pie, baked
1 package (8 ounces) reduced-fat cream cheese, softened
⅓ cup vanilla-flavored light nonfat yogurt
¼ cup EQUAL® SPOONFUL**
1 tablespoon lemon juice

*May substitute 1½ packets Equal® sweetener.

**May substitute 6 packets Equal® sweetener.

• Remove stems from several strawberries and slice to make 1 cup. Toss with 1 tablespoon Equal® Spoonful. Spread on bottom of baked pie shell.

• Beat cream cheese, yogurt, ¼ cup Equal® Spoonful and lemon juice until smooth and fluffy. Spread over sliced strawberries in pie shell. Remove stems from all but 1 large strawberry. Cut berries lengthwise in half. Place, cut side down, over cream cheese mixture, around outer edge of pie crust, with pointed end of berry facing center of pie. Make several thin slits in last whole berry starting near top and going to pointed end. Press gently with fingers to form "fan". Place in center of pie.

• Refrigerate pie at least 4 hours before serving.

Makes 8 servings

Nutrients per Serving:	
Calories:	185
Fat:	9 g
Protein:	4 g
Carbohydrate:	13 g
Cholesterol:	20 mg
Sodium:	144 mg

Dietary Exchanges: ½ Starch, ½ Fruit, 2 Fat

Cakes & Cheesecakes

Cool Lime Cheesecake

32% calorie reduction from traditional recipe

> 1 cup graham cracker crumbs
> 3 tablespoons stick butter or margarine, melted
> 2 tablespoons EQUAL® SPOONFUL*
> 2 packages (8 ounces each) reduced-fat cream cheese, softened
> ⅔ cup EQUAL® SPOONFUL**
> 1 egg
> 2 egg whites
> ½ teaspoon grated lime peel
> 3 tablespoons fresh lime juice

*May substitute 3 packets Equal® sweetener.

**May substitute 16 packets Equal® sweetener.

• Combine graham cracker crumbs, butter and 2 tablespoons Equal® Spoonful in bottom of 8-inch springform pan or 8-inch cake pan; pat evenly on bottom and ½ inch up side of pan. Bake in preheated 325°F oven 8 minutes.

• Beat cream cheese and ⅔ cup Equal® Spoonful in medium bowl until fluffy. Beat in egg, egg whites, lime peel and juice until well blended. Pour into prepared crust.

• Bake in 325°F oven 30 to 35 minutes or until center is almost set. Cool on wire rack. Refrigerate at least 3 hours before serving.

Makes 8 servings

Nutrients per Serving:	
Calories:	197
Fat:	11 g
Protein:	9 g
Carbohydrate:	14 g
Cholesterol:	58 mg
Sodium:	366 mg

Dietary Exchanges: 1 Milk, 2 Fat

New York Cheesecake

39% calorie reduction from traditional recipe

1¼ cups vanilla wafer crumbs
4 tablespoons stick butter or margarine, melted
2 tablespoons EQUAL® SPOONFUL*
3 packages (8 ounces each) reduced-fat cream cheese, softened
¾ cup EQUAL® SPOONFUL**
2 eggs
2 egg whites
2 tablespoons cornstarch
1 cup reduced-fat sour cream
1 teaspoon vanilla
1 pint strawberries, sliced (optional)

Strawberry Sauce (optional)
1 package (16 ounces) frozen unsweetened strawberries, thawed
¼ cup EQUAL® SPOONFUL***
1 tablespoon lemon juice

*May substitute 3 packets Equal® sweetener.

**May substitute 18 packets Equal® sweetener.

***May substitute 6 packets Equal® sweetener.

• Mix vanilla wafer crumbs, butter and 2 tablespoons Equal® Spoonful in bottom of 9-inch springform pan. Reserve 1 tablespoon of crumb mixture. Pat remaining mixture evenly on bottom and ½ inch up side of pan. Bake in preheated 325°F oven about 8 minutes or until crust is lightly browned. Cool on wire rack.

• Beat cream cheese and ¾ cup Equal® Spoonful in large bowl until fluffy; beat in eggs, egg whites and cornstarch. Mix in sour cream and vanilla until well blended. Pour mixture into crust in pan.

• Bake in 325°F oven 45 to 50 minutes or just until set in center. Remove cheesecake from oven, sprinkle with reserved crumbs. Cool completely on wire rack. Refrigerate 8 hours or overnight.

• For Strawberry Sauce, process strawberries in food processor or blender until smooth. Stir in ¼ cup Equal® Spoonful and lemon juice. Refrigerate until serving time.

• Remove side of springform pan; place cheesecake on serving plate. Serve with strawberries and Strawberry Sauce.

Makes 16 servings

Nutrients per Serving:

Calories:	158
Fat:	10g
Protein:	7g
Carbohydrate:	10g
Cholesterol:	50mg
Sodium:	234mg

Dietary Exchanges: 1 Milk, 2 Fat

Tip:

It's important to soften the cream cheese before beginning the recipe. It will then combine easily with other ingredients and prevent lumps from forming in the batter. To soften cream cheese quickly, remove the wrapper and place it on a medium microwave-safe plate. Microwave at MEDIUM (50% power) for 15 to 20 seconds or until slightly softened.

Mocha Swirl Cheesecake

48% calorie reduction from traditional recipe

>   1 cup chocolate wafer crumbs
>   ½ cup chopped pecans or almonds
>   3 tablespoons stick butter or margarine, melted
>   3 tablespoons EQUAL® SPOONFUL*
>   3 packages (8 ounces each) reduced-fat cream cheese,
>   softened
>   ¾ cup EQUAL® SPOONFUL**
>   2 eggs
>   2 egg whites
>   1½ tablespoons cornstarch
>   ¼ teaspoon salt
>   1 cup reduced-fat sour cream
>   2 teaspoons vanilla
>   3 tablespoons EQUAL® SPOONFUL***
>   1¼ teaspoons instant coffee crystals
>   1 teaspoon unsweetened cocoa powder

*May substitute 4½ packets Equal® sweetener.

**May substitute 18 packets Equal® sweetener.

***May substitute 4½ packets Equal® sweetener.

• Mix chocolate crumbs, pecans, butter and 3 tablespoons Equal® Spoonful in bottom of 9-inch springform pan. Pat mixture evenly onto bottom of pan; set aside while preparing filling.

• Beat cream cheese and ¾ cup Equal® Spoonful in large bowl until fluffy; beat in eggs, egg whites, cornstarch and salt. Beat in sour cream and vanilla until well blended.

• Remove ½ cup cheesecake batter. Stir in 3 tablespoons Equal® Spoonful, instant coffee crystals and cocoa until well combined. Pour half of plain batter into crust in pan. Top with 5 spoonfuls of coffee batter. Using tip of knife or spatula, gently swirl coffee batter into cheesecake. Repeat with remaining batters.

continued on page 72

Mocha Swirl Cheesecake, continued

• Bake in preheated 325°F oven 45 to 50 minutes or until center is almost set. Remove cheesecake to wire rack. Gently run metal spatula around rim of pan to loosen cake. Let cheesecake cool completely; cover and refrigerate several hours or overnight before serving. To serve, remove side of springform pan.

Makes 16 servings

Nutrients per Serving:	
Calories:	171
Fat:	12 g
Protein:	7 g
Carbohydrate:	9 g
Cholesterol:	56 mg
Sodium:	283 mg

Dietary Exchanges: 1 Milk, 2 Fat

Cranberry Orange Cheesecake

38% calorie reduction from traditional recipe

> 1⅓ cups gingersnap crumbs
> 3 tablespoons EQUAL® SPOONFUL*
> 3 tablespoons stick butter or margarine, melted
> 3 packages (8 ounces each) reduced-fat cream cheese, softened
> 1 cup EQUAL® SPOONFUL**
> 2 eggs
> 2 egg whites
> 2 tablespoons cornstarch
> ¼ teaspoon salt
> 1 cup reduced-fat sour cream
> 2 teaspoons vanilla
> 1 cup chopped fresh or frozen cranberries
> 1½ teaspoons grated orange peel

*May substitute 4½ packets Equal® sweetener.

**May substitute 24 packets Equal® sweetener.

• Mix gingersnap crumbs, 3 tablespoons Equal® Spoonful and melted butter in bottom of 9-inch springform pan. Reserve 2 tablespoons crumb mixture. Pat remaining mixture evenly onto bottom of pan. Bake in preheated 325°F oven 8 minutes. Cool on wire rack.

• Beat cream cheese and 1 cup Equal® Spoonful in large bowl until fluffy; beat in eggs, egg whites, cornstarch and salt. Beat in sour cream and vanilla until blended. Gently stir in cranberries and orange peel. Pour batter into crust in pan. Sprinkle with reserved crumb mixture.

• Bake in 325°F oven 45 to 50 minutes or until center is almost set. Remove cheesecake to wire rack. Gently run metal spatula around rim of pan to loosen cake. Let cheesecake cool completely; cover and refrigerate several hours or overnight before serving. To serve, remove side of springform pan.

Makes 16 servings

Nutrients per Serving:	
Calories:	196
Fat:	13 g
Protein:	7 g
Carbohydrate:	13 g
Cholesterol:	62 mg
Sodium:	268 mg

Dietary Exchanges: 1 Milk, 2½ Fat

Pineapple Upside-Down Cake

37% calorie reduction from traditional recipe

8 slices canned pineapple in juice, undrained
¼ cup EQUAL® SPOONFUL*
1 tablespoon stick butter or margarine, melted
1 tablespoon reserved pineapple juice
1 teaspoon cornstarch
4 maraschino cherries, drained, halved
2 tablespoons chopped nuts
1 cup EQUAL® SPOONFUL**
6 tablespoons stick butter or margarine, softened
2 eggs
1 teaspoon vanilla
1½ cups cake flour
1 teaspoon baking powder
½ teaspoon baking soda
½ teaspoon ground cinnamon
¼ teaspoon salt
⅓ cup buttermilk
⅓ cup reserved pineapple juice

*May substitute 6 packets Equal® sweetener.

**May substitute 24 packets Equal® sweetener.

• Drain pineapple slices, reserving juice. Combine ¼ cup Equal® Spoonful, melted butter, 1 tablespoon reserved pineapple juice and cornstarch in bottom of 9-inch round cake pan. Arrange drained pineapple slices, cherries and nuts over butter mixture.

• Beat 1 cup Equal® Spoonful, butter, eggs and vanilla with electric mixer until blended. Combine cake flour, baking powder, baking soda, cinnamon and salt. Add to butter mixture alternately with buttermilk and ⅓ cup reserved pineapple juice, beginning and ending with dry ingredients. Mix well after each addition. Spread batter over pineapple slices in pan.

• Bake in preheated 350°F oven 20 to 25 minutes or until wooden pick inserted in center comes out clean. Let stand a few minutes, then invert onto serving plate. Serve warm or at room temperature. *Makes 8 servings*

continued on page 76

Pineapple Upside-Down Cake, continued

Nutrients per Serving:	
Calories:	261
Fat:	13 g
Protein:	5 g
Carbohydrate:	32 g
Cholesterol:	81 mg
Sodium:	342 mg

Dietary Exchanges: 1 Starch, 1 Fruit, 2½ Fat

Bittersweet Chocolate Torte

46% calorie reduction from traditional recipe

Torte
> 6 tablespoons stick butter or margarine
> 4 ounces unsweetened chocolate
> ⅓ cup fat-free milk
> ⅓ cup sugar-free apricot preserves or apricot spreadable
>   fruit
> 2 teaspoons instant coffee crystals
> 1 egg yolk
> 1 teaspoon vanilla
> 1½ cups EQUAL® SPOONFUL*
> 3 egg whites
> ⅛ teaspoon cream of tartar
> ¼ cup all-purpose flour
> ⅛ teaspoon salt

Rich Chocolate Glaze
> 1 ounce semi-sweet chocolate
> 1 tablespoon stick butter or margarine
>   Whipped topping, fresh raspberries and/or fresh mint
>   (optional)

*May substitute 36 packets Equal® sweetener.

• For Torte, heat 6 tablespoons butter, 4 ounces unsweetened chocolate, milk, preserves and coffee crystals in small saucepan, whisking frequently until chocolate is almost melted.

• Remove pan from heat; continue whisking until chocolate is melted and mixture is smooth. Whisk in egg yolk and vanilla; add Equal®, whisking until smooth.

• Lightly grease bottom of 8-inch cake pan and line with parchment or waxed paper. Beat egg whites and cream of tartar to stiff peaks in large bowl. Fold chocolate mixture into egg whites; fold in combined flour and salt. Pour cake batter into prepared pan.

• Bake in preheated 350°F oven 20 to 25 minutes or until wooden pick inserted in center comes out clean. Do not overbake. Carefully loosen side of cake from pan with small sharp knife, which will keep cake from cracking as it cools. Cool cake completely in pan on wire rack; refrigerate 1 to 2 hours or until chilled.

• For Rich Chocolate Glaze, melt 1 ounce semi-sweet chocolate and 1 tablespoon butter in small saucepan, stirring frequently.

• Remove cake from pan and place on serving plate. Pour Rich Chocolate Glaze over top of cake, letting it run down sides. Let cake stand about 1 hour or until glaze is set. Garnish top of cake with whipped topping, fresh raspberries and fresh mint.

Makes 12 servings

Nutrients per Serving:	
Calories:	145
Fat:	12 g
Protein:	3 g
Carbohydrate:	9 g
Cholesterol:	36 mg
Sodium:	116 mg

Dietary Exchanges: ½ Starch, 2 Fat

Rich Chocolate Cheesecake

35% calorie reduction from traditional recipe

>   1 cup chocolate wafer crumbs
>   3 tablespoons EQUAL® SPOONFUL*
>   3 tablespoons stick butter or margarine, melted
>   3 packages (8 ounces each) reduced-fat cream cheese,
>   softened
>   1¼ cups EQUAL® SPOONFUL**
>   2 eggs
>   2 egg whites
>   2 tablespoons cornstarch
>   ¼ teaspoon salt
>   1 cup reduced-fat sour cream
>   2 teaspoons vanilla
>   4 ounces (4 squares) semi-sweet chocolate, melted and
>   slightly cooled

*May substitute 4½ packets Equal® sweetener.

**May substitute 30 packets Equal® sweetener.

• Mix chocolate crumbs, 3 tablespoons Equal® Spoonful and melted butter in bottom of 9-inch springform pan. Pat mixture evenly onto bottom of pan. Bake in preheated 325°F oven 8 minutes. Cool on wire rack.

• Beat cream cheese and 1¼ cups Equal® Spoonful in large bowl until fluffy; beat in eggs, egg whites, cornstarch and salt. Beat in sour cream and vanilla until well blended. Gently fold in melted chocolate. Pour batter into crust.

• Bake in 325°F oven 40 to 45 minutes or until center is almost set. Remove cheesecake to wire rack. Gently run metal spatula around rim of pan to loosen cake. Let cheesecake cool completely; cover and refrigerate several hours or overnight before serving. To serve, remove side of springform pan.

Makes 16 servings

continued on page 80

Rich Chocolate Cheesecake, continued

Nutrients per Serving:	
Calories:	217
Fat:	16g
Protein:	7g
Carbohydrate:	13g
Cholesterol:	62mg
Sodium:	246mg

Dietary Exchanges: 1 Milk, 3 Fat

Peach Almond Upside-Down Cake

36% calorie reduction from traditional recipe

  1 can (15 ounces) sliced light peaches in light syrup, undrained
¼ cup EQUAL® SPOONFUL*
  3 tablespoons sugar-free apricot preserves or apricot spreadable fruit
  1 tablespoon stick butter or margarine, melted
  1 tablespoon reserved peach syrup
  2 tablespoons sliced toasted almonds
  1 cup EQUAL® SPOONFUL**
  6 tablespoons stick butter or margarine, softened
  2 eggs
  ¾ teaspoon almond extract
1½ cups cake flour
  1 teaspoon baking powder
  ½ teaspoon baking soda
  ¼ teaspoon salt
  ¼ teaspoon ground cinnamon
  ⅓ cup buttermilk
  ⅓ cup reserved peach syrup

*May substitute 6 packets Equal® sweetener.

**May substitute 24 packets Equal® sweetener.

• Drain peaches, reserving syrup. Combine ¼ cup Equal® Spoonful, preserves, melted butter and 1 tablespoon reserved peach syrup in bottom of 9-inch round cake pan. Cut peach slices horizontally in half. Arrange slices in concentric circles over butter mixture. Sprinkle with almonds.

• Beat 1 cup Equal® Spoonful, softened butter, eggs and almond extract with electric mixer until blended. Combine cake flour, baking powder, baking soda, salt and cinnamon. Add to butter mixture alternately with buttermilk and ⅓ cup reserved peach syrup, beginning and ending with dry ingredients. Mix well after each addition. Spread batter over peach slices in pan.

• Bake in preheated 350°F oven 20 to 25 minutes or until wooden pick inserted in center comes out clean. Let stand a few minutes, then invert onto serving plate. Serve warm or at room temperature.   *Makes 8 servings*

Nutrients per Serving:	
Calories:	253
Fat:	12 g
Protein:	4 g
Carbohydrate:	30 g
Cholesterol:	81 mg
Sodium:	347 mg

Dietary Exchanges: 1 Starch, 1 Fruit, 2 Fat

Tip:

Toasting nuts before using them intensifies their flavor and crunch. To toast nuts, spread them on a baking sheet and place in a 350°F oven for 8 to 10 minutes. Or, toast nuts in an ungreased skillet over medium heat until golden brown, stirring frequently. Always cool nuts to room temperature before combining them with other ingredients.

More Desserts

Cranberry Apple Crisp

59% calorie reduction from traditional recipe

> 3 cups peeled and sliced apples
> 2 cups fresh cranberries
> 1 cup EQUAL® SPOONFUL*
> ½ cup EQUAL® SPOONFUL**
> ⅓ cup all-purpose flour
> ¼ cup chopped pecans
> ¼ cup stick butter or margarine, melted

*May substitute 24 packets Equal® sweetener.

**May substitute 12 packets Equal® sweetener.

• Combine apples, cranberries and 1 cup Equal® Spoonful in ungreased 10-inch pie pan.

• Combine ½ cup Equal® Spoonful, flour, pecans and butter in separate bowl. Sprinkle mixture over top of apples and cranberries.

• Bake in preheated 350°F oven about 1 hour or until bubbly and lightly browned. *Makes 8 servings*

Tip: This crisp is delicious served as an accompaniment to pork or poultry or with frozen yogurt as a dessert.

Nutrients per Serving:	
Calories:	145
Fat:	8 g
Protein:	1 g
Carbohydrate:	18 g
Cholesterol:	16 mg
Sodium:	67 mg

Dietary Exchanges: 1 Fruit, 1½ Fat

Creamy Rice Pudding

49% calorie reduction from traditional recipe

2 cups water
1 cinnamon stick, broken into pieces
1 cup converted rice
4 cups fat-free milk
¼ teaspoon salt
1 cup EQUAL® SPOONFUL*
2 eggs
1 egg yolk
1 teaspoon vanilla
¼ cup raisins
Ground cinnamon and nutmeg

May substitute 24 packets Equal® sweetener.

• Heat water and cinnamon stick to a boil in large saucepan; stir in rice. Reduce heat and simmer, covered, 20 to 25 minutes or until rice is tender and water is absorbed. Discard cinnamon.

• Stir in milk and salt; heat to a boil. Reduce heat and simmer, covered, about 15 to 20 minutes or until mixture starts to thicken, stirring frequently. (Milk will not be absorbed and pudding will thicken when it cools.) Remove from heat and cool 1 to 2 minutes; stir in Equal®.

• Beat whole eggs, egg yolk and vanilla in small bowl until blended. Stir about ½ cup rice mixture into egg mixture; stir back into saucepan. Cook over low heat, stirring constantly, 1 to 2 minutes. Stir in raisins.

• Spoon pudding into serving bowl; sprinkle with cinnamon and nutmeg. Serve warm or at room temperature.

Makes 6 (⅔-cup) servings

Nutrients per Serving:	
Calories:	244
Fat:	3g
Protein:	11g
Carbohydrate:	43g
Cholesterol:	109mg
Sodium:	200mg

Dietary Exchanges: 2 Starch, 1 Milk, ½ Fat

Rhubarb and Apple Crumble

36% calorie reduction from traditional recipe

> 3 cups ¾-inch cubed and peeled Granny Smith apples
> (about 3 medium)
> 2½ cups ¾-inch cubed fresh red rhubarb
> ½ cup EQUAL® SPOONFUL*
> 2 tablespoons cornstarch
> ⅓ cup water or apple juice
> 1 tablespoon lemon juice
> 1 teaspoon grated lemon peel (optional)
> ¾ cup quick or old-fashioned oats, uncooked
> ⅓ cup EQUAL® SPOONFUL**
> ¼ cup raisins
> ¼ cup chopped nuts
> 2 tablespoons stick butter or margarine, melted
> ½ to ¾ teaspoon cinnamon

*May substitute 12 packets Equal® sweetener.

**May substitute 8 packets Equal® sweetener.

• Combine apples, rhubarb, ½ cup Equal® Spoonful and cornstarch. Place in 1½-quart casserole dish.

• Combine water, lemon juice and lemon peel. Pour over fruit mixture. Cover and bake in preheated 400°F oven 20 to 25 minutes or until fruit is tender.

• Meanwhile, combine oats, ⅓ cup Equal® Spoonful, raisins, nuts, butter and cinnamon until well blended. Remove cover from fruit mixture. Sprinkle with oats mixture. Return to oven and bake, uncovered, an additional 8 to 10 minutes or until topping is crisp.

• Serve warm with frozen yogurt, ice cream or whipped topping.

Makes 6 servings

Nutrients per Serving:	
Calories:	177
Fat:	8g
Protein:	3g
Carbohydrate:	26g
Cholesterol:	10mg
Sodium:	45mg
Dietary Exchanges: 1 Starch, 1 Fruit, 1½ Fat	

Baked Cinnamon Applesauce

18% calorie reduction from traditional recipe

> 1 orange
> 1 lemon
> 3 pounds Granny Smith apples, peeled, cored and quartered
> 3 pounds Royal Gala or Braeburn apples, peeled, cored and quartered
> 3 tablespoons stick butter or margarine, cut into small pieces
> 2 teaspoons ground cinnamon
> ¼ teaspoon ground nutmeg
> ½ cup EQUAL® SPOONFUL*

*May substitute 12 packets Equal® sweetener.

• Grate peel of orange and lemon. Place in 3-quart glass or non-corrosive casserole with cover. Squeeze juice from orange and lemon; add to grated peel in casserole. Add apples, butter, cinnamon and nutmeg. Toss to combine.

• Cover with casserole lid. Bake in preheated 350°F oven 1½ hours. Remove from oven and let stand, covered, 30 minutes. Carefully remove lid. Stir to break up apples; stir in Equal®. Serve warm or refrigerate, covered, several hours before serving.   *Makes 12 (½-cup) servings*

Nutrients per Serving:	
Calories:	129
Fat:	3 g
Protein:	0 g
Carbohydrate:	27 g
Cholesterol:	8 mg
Sodium:	1 mg

Dietary Exchanges: 2 Fruit, ½ Fat

Pumpkin Raisin Muffins

32% calorie reduction from traditional recipe

¾ cup canned pumpkin
6 tablespoons vegetable oil
1 egg
2 egg whites
1 tablespoon light molasses
2 teaspoons vanilla
1¼ cups all-purpose flour
1 cup EQUAL® SPOONFUL*
½ cup raisins
1 tablespoon baking powder
1 teaspoon ground cinnamon
½ teaspoon ground nutmeg
½ teaspoon ground ginger
¼ teaspoon salt

May substitute 24 packets Equal® sweetener.

• Combine pumpkin, oil, egg, egg whites, molasses and vanilla. Stir in combined flour, Equal®, raisins, baking powder, cinnamon, nutmeg, ginger and salt just until all ingredients are moistened. Fill paper-lined 2½-inch muffin cups about ¾ full.

• Bake in preheated 375°F oven 18 to 20 minutes or until wooden toothpick inserted in center comes out clean. Cool in pan on wire rack 2 to 3 minutes. Remove muffins from pan and cool completely on wire rack.   *Makes 12 muffins*

Nutrients per Serving:	
Calories:	149
Fat:	8 g
Protein:	3 g
Carbohydrate:	18 g
Cholesterol:	18 mg
Sodium:	224 mg

Dietary Exchanges: 1 Starch, 1½ Fat

Pumpkin Raisin Muffin

Cinnamon Raisin Bread Pudding

34% calorie reduction from traditional recipe

>   2 cups fat-free milk
>   ⅔ cup EQUAL® SPOONFUL*
>   4 tablespoons stick butter or margarine, melted
>   1 egg
>   2 egg whites
>   1 teaspoon ground cinnamon
>   ¼ teaspoon salt
>   4 cups day-old cinnamon raisin bread (¾-inch cubes)

May substitute 16 packets Equal® sweetener.

• Combine milk, Equal®, melted butter, egg, egg whites, cinnamon and salt in large bowl. Stir in bread cubes.

• Spoon mixture into ungreased 1½-quart rectangular casserole. Bake in preheated 350°F oven 30 to 35 minutes or until pudding is set and sharp knife inserted near center comes out clean.

Makes 6 servings

Nutrients per Serving:	
Calories:	232
Fat:	10 g
Protein:	10 g
Carbohydrate:	26 g
Cholesterol:	37 mg
Sodium:	405 mg

Dietary Exchanges: 1½ Starch, ½ Milk, 2 Fat

EQUAL SWEETENER

Gingerbread Muffins

32% calorie reduction from traditional recipe

1½ cups all-purpose flour
2 cups Kellogg's® Special K® cereal, crushed to 1 cup
¾ cup EQUAL® SPOONFUL*
½ cup raisins
1 tablespoon baking powder
1 teaspoon ground cinnamon
½ teaspoon ground ginger
¼ teaspoon ground cloves
¼ teaspoon baking soda
¼ teaspoon salt
1 cup low-fat buttermilk
2 egg whites
2 tablespoons vegetable oil
3 tablespoons light molasses

May substitute 18 packets Equal® sweetener.

• Combine flour, crushed cereal, Equal®, raisins, baking powder, cinnamon, ginger, cloves, baking soda and salt in large mixing bowl.

• Stir in buttermilk, egg whites, vegetable oil and molasses just until all ingredients are moistened. Fill paper-lined 2½-inch muffin cups ⅔ full.

• Bake in preheated 400°F oven 18 to 20 minutes or until wooden pick inserted in center comes out clean. Cool in pan on wire rack 2 to 3 minutes. Remove muffins from pan and serve warm or at room temperature.   *Makes 12 muffins*

Nutrients per Serving:	
Calories:	152
Fat:	4 g
Protein:	4 g
Carbohydrate:	26 g
Cholesterol:	1 mg
Sodium:	273 mg

Dietary Exchanges: 2 Starch, ½ Fat

Index

Apples
Apple Raisin Oatmeal Cookies, 48
Apple Streusel Pie, 58
Baked Cinnamon Applesauce, 87
Cranberry Apple Crisp, 82
Rhubarb and Apple Crumble, 86
Tangy Apple Slaw, 32

Baked Cinnamon Applesauce, 87
Bananas
Fruit Smoothies, 14
Soy Milk Smoothie, 10
Bar Cookies
Double Chocolate Brownies, 44
Peanut Butter Chocolate Bars, 46
Berries
Blueberry Pie, 52
Fresh Strawberry Cream Pie, 64
Fruit Smoothies, 14
Nectarine and Berry Pie, 56
Soy Milk Smoothie, 10
Strawberry Limeade, 22
Triple-Berry Jam, 18
Beverages
Coffee Latte, 20
Cranberry-Lime Margarita Punch,
   8
Fruit Smothies, 10
Irish Cream Iced Cappuccino, 16
Lemonade, 21
Soy Milk Smoothie, 10
Strawberry Limeade, 22
Bittersweet Chocolate Torte, 76
Blueberry Pie, 52
Breads
Gingerbread Muffins, 92
Pumpkin Raisin Muffins, 88

Cakes
Bittersweet Chocolate Torte, 74
Peach Almond Upside-Down Cake,
   80
Pineapple Upside-Down Cake, 74
Cheesecakes
Cool Lime Cheesecake, 66
Cranberry Orange Cheesecake,
   72
Mocha Swirl Cheesecake, 70
New York Cheesecake, 68
Rich Chocolate Cheesecake, 78

Chocolate
Bittersweet Chocolate Torte, 76
Chocolate Chip Cookies, 42
Double Chocolate Brownies, 44
Mocha Swirl Cheesecake, 68
Peanut Butter Chocolate Bars, 46
Pumpkin Polka Dot Cookies, 50
Rich Chocolate Cheesecake, 78
Special Crunchy Cookies, 49
Cinnamon Equal®, 20
Cinnamon Raisin Bread Pudding,
   90
Citrus Bean Salad, 37
Coffee
Bittersweet Chocolate Torte, 74
Coffee Latte, 20
Irish Cream Iced Cappuccino, 16
Mocha Swirl Cheesecake, 68
Cookies
Apple Raisin Oatmeal Cookies, 48
Chocolate Chip Cookies, 40
Orange Cranberry Cookies, 45
Pumpkin Polka Dot Cookies, 48
Special Crunchy Cookies, 49
Cool Lime Cheesecake, 66
Country Peach Tart, 55
Cranberries
Cranberry Apple Crisp, 82
Cranberry-Lime Margarita Punch, 8
Cranberry Orange Cheesecake, 72
Cranberry Salad, 26
Orange Cranberry Cookies, 45
Creamy Rice Pudding, 84
Cucumber Tomato Salad, 24

Desserts
Baked Cinnamon Applesauce, 87
Cinnamon Raisin Bread Pudding,
   90
Cranberry Apple Crisp, 82
Creamy Rice Pudding, 84
Rhubarb and Apple Crumble, 86
Double Chocolate Brownies, 44

Entrées
Gingered Chicken with Vegetables,
   28
Ham with Cherry Sauce, 31
Southern Style Mustard BBQ
   Chicken Kabobs, 34

Equal® Cinnamon Cream Cheese, 12

Fresh Strawberry Cream Pie, 64
Fruit Smoothies, 14

Gingerbread Muffins, 92
Gingered Chicken with Vegetables, 28

Ham with Cherry Sauce, 27

Irish Cream Iced Cappuccino, 16

Lemonade, 21
Lemon Meringue Pie, 60

Marinated Carrot Salad, 30
Mocha Swirl Cheesecake, 68

Nectarine and Berry Pie, 56
New York Cheesecake, 66

Oats
  Apple Raisin Oatmeal Cookies, 48
  Orange Cranberry Cookies, 45
  Peanut Butter Chocolate Bars, 46
  Rhubarb and Apple Crumble, 86
Orange Cranberry Cookies, 45

Peach Almond Upside-Down Cake, 80
Peach Freezer Jam, 15
Peanut Butter Chocolate Bars, 46
Pies
  Apple Streusel Pie, 58
  Blueberry Pie, 52
  Fresh Strawberry Cream Pie, 64
  Lemon Meringue Pie, 60
  Nectarine and Berry Pie, 56
  Pumpkin Pie, 63
  Sweet Potato Pie, 54
Pineapple
  Cranberry Salad, 26
  Pineapple Upside-Down Cake, 74
  Sweet and Sour Carrots, 38
Pumpkin
  Pumpkin Pie, 63
  Pumpkin Polka Dot Cookies, 50
  Pumpkin Raisin Muffins, 88

Raisins
  Apple Raisin Oatmeal Cookies, 48
  Cinnamon Raisin Bread Pudding, 90
  Creamy Rice Pudding, 84
  Gingerbread Muffins, 92
  Pumpkin Raisin Muffins, 88
  Reunion Salad, 36
  Rhubarb and Apple Crumble, 86
Reunion Salad, 36
Rhubarb and Apple Crumble, 86
Rich Chocolate Cheesecake, 78

Salads
  Citrus Bean Salad, 37
  Cranberry Salad, 26
  Cucumber Tomato Salad, 24
  Marinated Carrot Salad, 30
  Reunion Salad, 36
  Tangy Apple Slaw, 32
  Thai Broccoli Salad, 40
Southern Style Mustard BBQ Chicken Kabobs, 34
Soy Milk Smoothie, 10
Special Crunchy Cookies, 49
Spreads
  Equal® Cinnamon Cream Cheese, 12
  Peach Freezer Jam, 15
  Triple-Berry Jam, 18
Strawberry Limeade, 22
Sweet and Sour Carrots, 38
Sweet Potato Pie, 54

Tangy Apple Slaw, 32
Tarts: Country Peach Tart, 55
Thai Broccoli Salad, 40
Triple-Berry Jam, 18